Table of Contents

Preface: _____ 5

Introduction: The Key to Thriving Workplaces _____ 7

Chapter 1: Setting the Foundation for Wellness _____ 13

Chapter 2: Communication for Wellness _____ 19

Chapter 3: Building Resilience in the Workplace _____ 27

Chapter 4: The Role of Routine and Boundaries _____ 35

Chapter 5: Cultivating Connection and Support _____ 43

Chapter 6: Recognition and Validation _____ 51

Chapter 7: Wellness-Focused Policies and Benefits _____ 59

Chapter 8: Leadership's Role in Wellness _____ 67

Chapter 9: Measuring and Sustaining Wellness _____ 75

Conclusion: A Call to Action for Wellness _____ 85

WORKPLACE WELLNESS
BALANCING WORK AND MENTAL HEALTH

OMRAN KHAYAMI

Copyright © 2024. All rights reserved.
No part of this book may be reproduced, distributed, or transmitted in any form or by any means, including photocopying, recording, or other electronic or mechanical methods, without the prior written permission of the author, except for brief excerpts in critical reviews or analyses.

Preface:

"Workplace Wellness: Balancing Work and Mental Health" emerges from a deep-seated belief that the health of an organization hinges not merely on the strategies it employs or the technologies it adopts, but fundamentally on the wellness of its people.

In an era where burnout, stress, and job dissatisfaction are all too common, this book offers a fresh perspective, one that places the mental, emotional, and physical health of employees at the forefront of business success. Each chapter delves into practical, actionable insights that draw on the latest research and real-world applications from organizations leading the way in employee wellness.

My journey in writing this book was inspired by my own experiences and the stories of countless others who have faced workplace challenges that impacted their health and happiness. It became clear that change wasn't just necessary—it was imperative for the sustainability of both individuals and their organizations.

"Workplace Wellness" is structured to guide HR professionals, managers, and employees alike through the essential components of crafting a supportive work environment. From establishing a foundation of wellness, through strategies for communication and resilience, to leadership's pivotal role in cultivating a culture of health, this book provides a comprehensive roadmap.

As you embark on this journey with me, I invite you to reflect on the transformative power of wellness in the workplace. This is not just about preventing burnout or reducing turnover; it's about creating a vibrant, engaging, and supportive workplace where every person can thrive. The goal is simple yet ambitious: to redefine the workplace so that wellness becomes as integral to your organization as any business strategy.

INTRODUCTION: THE KEY TO THRIVING WORKPLACES

Introduction: The Key to Thriving Workplaces

In today's fast-paced, ever-changing world, the line between work and life has blurred, often at the expense of our mental, physical, and emotional well-being. Now more than ever, the need for workplace wellness isn't just a trending topic—it's a critical foundation for success.

Imagine a workplace where employees wake up each morning excited to contribute, where leaders actively champion mental health, and where policies and practices support a healthy balance between ambition and self-care. This isn't just an aspirational vision; it's an attainable reality.

Workplace Wellness: Balancing Work and Mental Health isn't about quick fixes or adding trendy perks. It's about creating environments where people can thrive—where they feel supported, valued, and empowered to bring their best selves to work every day.

The Growing Need for Workplace Wellness

The global workforce is experiencing a wellness revolution. With the rise of hybrid work models, shifting employee expectations, and increasing awareness of mental health challenges, organizations can no longer afford to ignore the well-being of their people.

Research consistently shows that wellness-focused workplaces:

| Experience higher employee engagement | Benefit from reduced absenteeism | Promote greater innovation and collaboration |

Yet, many organizations struggle to define and implement meaningful wellness strategies. Some introduce initiatives without understanding employee needs, while others fail to integrate wellness into the broader workplace culture. This gap is precisely what this book aims to address.

Workplace Wellness is your comprehensive guide to creating a thriving work environment where employees aren't just surviving—they're flourishing.

The Ripple Effect of Wellness

The impact of workplace wellness extends far beyond the office. When employees feel supported at work, they carry that positivity into their personal lives, strengthening families and uplifting communities. Conversely, workplaces that neglect wellness risk perpetuating cycles of stress, burnout, and disengagement.

Imagine Fatima, a project manager at a Bahraini logistics firm. Before her company introduced flexible hours and mindfulness sessions, she struggled to balance her demanding workload with family responsibilities. After adopting wellness-focused practices, Fatima reported feeling less stressed and more productive. Her renewed energy transformed her team dynamics and improved her personal relationships—a ripple effect that underscores the profound impact of prioritizing wellness.

This book will show you how to create such transformative outcomes in your own organization.

What This Book Offers

Workplace Wellness goes beyond theories and frameworks. It's a practical toolkit designed to help leaders, HR professionals, and employees turn wellness ideas into action. Each chapter dives deep into essential aspects of workplace wellness, including:

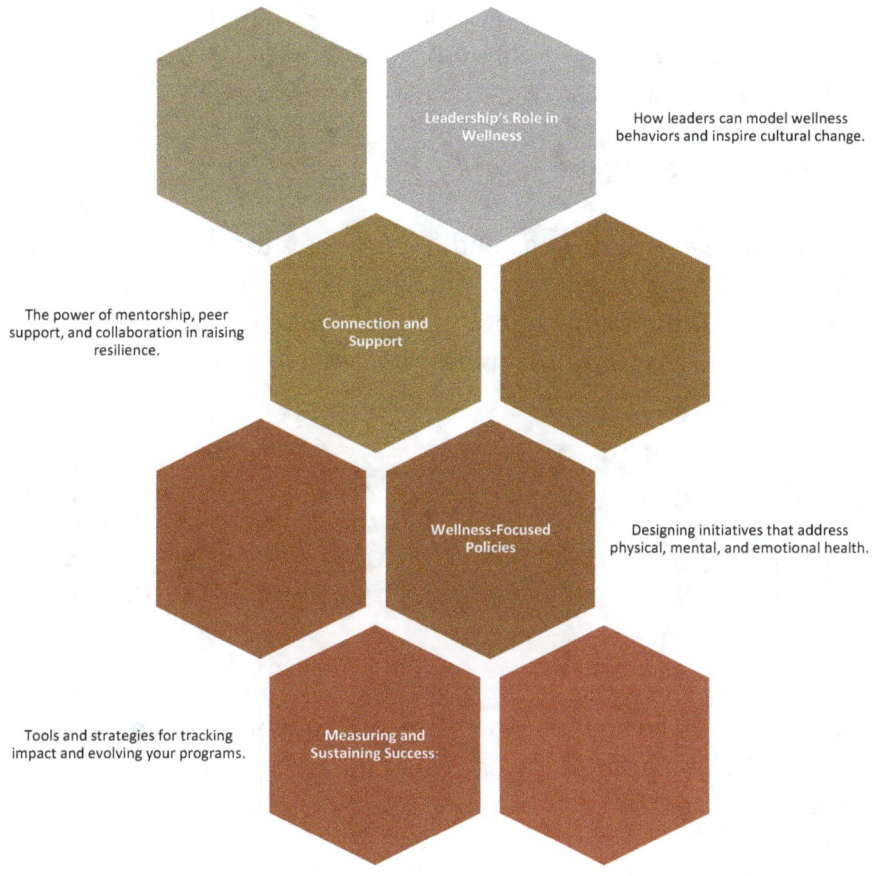

Every chapter combines actionable strategies, real-life success stories, and inspirational insights to guide you on this journey.

A Shared Responsibility

Workplace wellness isn't the sole responsibility of leaders or HR—it's a shared effort. It requires active participation and commitment from every level of the organization. When leaders champion wellness, teams collaborate to support one another, and individuals take ownership of their well-being, the results are transformative.

This book emphasizes that wellness is not a one-size-fits-all solution. Whether you're leading a global corporation or a small family business, the principles outlined here can be tailored to meet your unique needs and goals.

Your Role in Shaping the Future

The workplace is evolving, and you are at the forefront of this change. By reading this book, you've taken the first step toward creating a healthier, happier, and more productive work environment. As you embark on this journey, remember:

Change starts with small, consistent actions	Wellness is a journey, not a destination	Most successful wellness initiatives reflect the values and needs of your people

Together, we can redefine what it means to work well and live well. Let this book be your guide as you build a workplace that inspires, supports, and empowers everyone it touches.

Let's Get Started

Whether you're a leader, an HR professional, or an employee, this book is for you. As you turn the pages, you'll find practical tools, actionable steps, and inspirational stories that will help you transform your workplace into a hub of wellness and productivity.

The time to act is now. Let's create workplaces where people don't just work—they thrive.

Introduction: The Key to Thriving Workplaces | 11

1 SETTING THE FOUNDATION FOR WELLNESS

Chapter 1: Setting the Foundation for Wellness

Introduction: Creating the Bedrock of Thriving Workplaces

Wellness begins with intention. It's not something that happens by accident—it's built, brick by brick, on the foundation of a supportive environment, clear priorities, and proactive measures. A workplace that prioritizes wellness doesn't just survive challenges—it thrives through them, cultivates a culture where employees feel empowered and engaged.

In this chapter, we'll explore the fundamental elements of establishing a wellness-centered workplace. From creating a positive environment to embedding wellness into organizational culture, this chapter lays the groundwork for success.

The Role of Environment in Workplace Wellness

Physical Environment: More Than Just a Workspace

The physical environment plays a critical role in employee well-being. A thoughtfully designed workspace can reduce stress, boost productivity, and improve morale.

Key Elements to Consider:

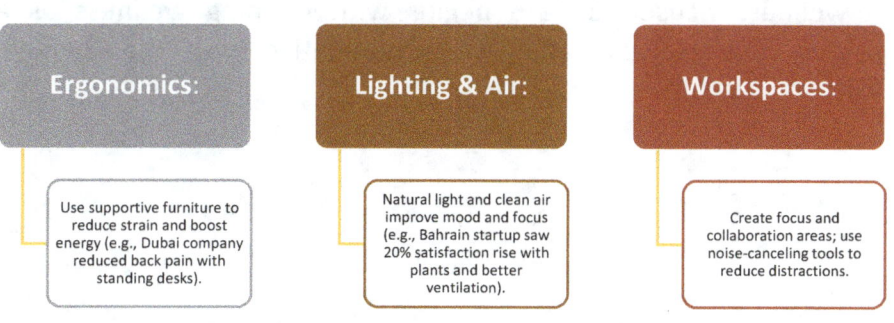

Psychological Environment: Nurturing Trust and Safety

The psychological environment is equally crucial. Employees need to feel emotionally safe and valued to perform at their best.

Strategies to Enhance Psychological Safety:

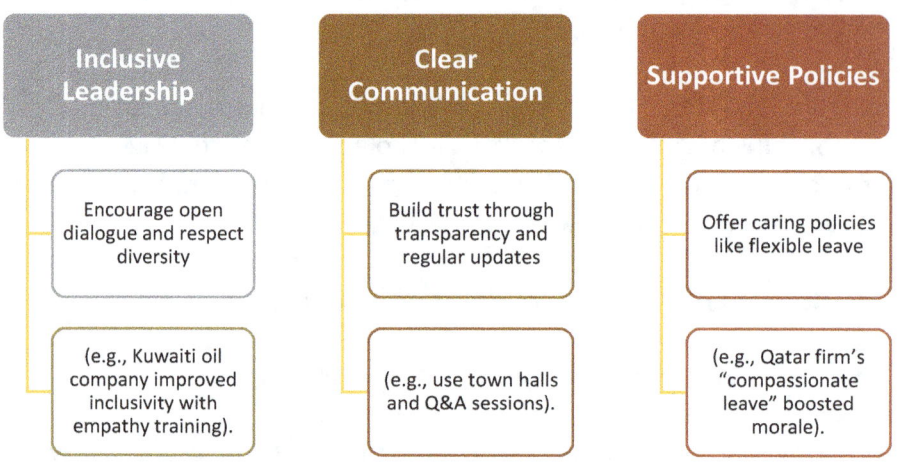

Building a Wellness-Centric Culture

Defining Wellness as a Core Value

A wellness-focused culture begins with defining wellness as a priority. This involves aligning wellness initiatives with organizational values and goals.

Steps to Embed Wellness:

Encouraging Daily Wellness Practices

Small, consistent actions create long-term change. Organizations can promote daily habits that prioritize well-being.

Ideas for Daily Wellness Practices:

Engaging Employees in Wellness

Building Ownership and Participation

Chapter 1: Setting the Foundation for Wellness | 15

Employees are more likely to embrace wellness initiatives when they feel involved in their creation.

Ways to Promote Engagement:

Real-Life Success Stories

A Thriving Office in Oman

Faced with declining morale, a telecommunications company in Oman reimagined its approach to wellness. They:

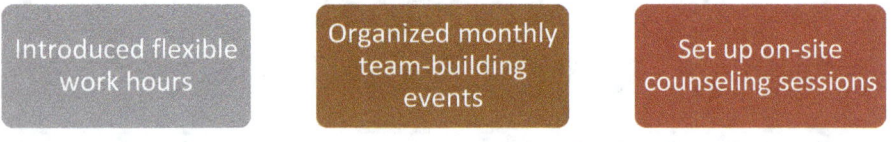

Results: Within a year, employee engagement scores rose by **40%**, and absenteeism decreased significantly.

A Resilient Team in Bahrain

When a Bahrain-based tech startup noticed rising burnout, they launched a "Recharge Thursdays" initiative, where employees could leave early to focus on personal wellness. The initiative led to:

| Improved productivity | Stronger team cohesion |

Practical Action Plan: Laying the Foundation

To create a wellness-first workplace, start with these foundational steps:

Evaluate	Set Goals	Launch	Communicate
• Assess environments to identify improvements	• Define success metrics like participation or absenteeism	• Pilot initiatives like mindfulness workshops or quiet zones	• Share the vision and early successes to build momentum

Closing Thoughts

Building a wellness foundation is an investment in your people and your organization's future. By creating an environment where employees feel supported and valued, you set the stage for innovation, collaboration, and sustained success.

Takeaway Challenge: This week, identify one small change you can make to improve your workplace environment—whether it's introducing a mindfulness practice, enhancing communication, or creating a quiet workspace. Take the first step toward building a foundation for wellness.

2 COMMUNICATION FOR WELLNESS

Chapter 2: Communication for Wellness

Introduction: The Power of Words in Wellness

Communication is the backbone of any workplace. It builds relationships, forwards collaboration, and resolves conflicts. But when communication falters, so does wellness. Poor communication can create stress, misunderstandings, and disconnection, while thoughtful, empathetic communication enhances trust, reduces anxiety, and strengthens team bonds.

This chapter explores how communication impacts workplace wellness and provides actionable strategies for adopting open, empathetic, and effective communication at all levels.

Why Communication Matters for Wellness

The Impact on Mental Health

Communication directly influences how employees feel about their work and workplace. Misunderstandings, unclear instructions, or a lack of acknowledgment can lead to frustration, stress, and burnout. On the other hand, open and empathetic communication creates an environment of trust, making employees feel valued and understood.

Example:
In a Bahrain-based tech company, a manager who began practicing active listening during team meetings noticed improved morale and productivity. Employees felt heard and were more open to sharing their challenges, leading to quicker resolutions and stronger collaboration.

Building Empathetic Communication Skills

1. Active Listening

Active listening involves fully concentrating on what the speaker is saying, understanding their message, and responding thoughtfully. It is a cornerstone of effective communication.

Strategies for Active Listening:

- Maintain eye contact to show attentiveness
- Paraphrase the speaker's message to confirm understanding
- Use phrases like, "It sounds like you're saying..." to validate their feelings

Example:
At a logistics company in Dubai, team leaders who practiced active listening during one-on-one check-ins reported a significant drop in workplace conflicts and an improvement in employee satisfaction scores.

2. Emotional Intelligence in Communication

Emotional intelligence (EQ) is the ability to understand and manage your emotions and recognize and influence the emotions of others. High EQ nurtures empathy, patience, and clarity in workplace interactions.

How to Enhance EQ:

- Practice self-awareness by reflecting on your emotional responses
- Use empathy to understand others' perspectives
- Regulate emotions by pausing before responding in challenging situations

Pro Tip:

In moments of tension, ask yourself, "What is this person feeling, and how can I address it constructively?"

Strategies for Effective Communication in Teams

1. Clarity and Transparency

Clear communication minimizes misunderstandings and sets realistic expectations. Transparency builds trust and encourages a culture of openness.

Practical Steps for Clear Communication:

- Use direct language without jargon
- Provide written follow-ups for verbal instructions
- Encourage questions to clarify uncertainties

Example:
In a Kuwaiti oil company, managers began using standardized templates for project updates, ensuring consistency and clarity across departments. This reduced project delays and improved cross-team collaboration.

2. The Role of Feedback

Feedback is a powerful tool for growth when delivered thoughtfully. It can reinforce positive behaviors, address areas for improvement, and show employees that their contributions are noticed.

How to Give Effective Feedback:

- 1. Start with positives to create a constructive tone
- 2. Be specific about what went well or needs improvement
- 3. End with actionable suggestions and offer support

Example:
A team in Oman introduced weekly "feedback circles," where employees shared one positive observation and one area of growth with a colleague. This initiative raised mutual respect and accountability.

3. Nonverbal Communication

Nonverbal cues, such as body language and tone of voice, play a significant role in communication. Misaligned verbal and nonverbal signals can create confusion or mistrust.

Tips for Positive Nonverbal Communication:

- 1. Maintain an open posture to appear approachable
- 2. Smile and nod to show engagement
- 3. Use a calm, steady tone of voice during discussions

Digital Communication and Wellness

In an increasingly remote and hybrid work environment, digital communication requires extra care to ensure messages are clear, respectful, and supportive.

Best Practices for Digital Communication:

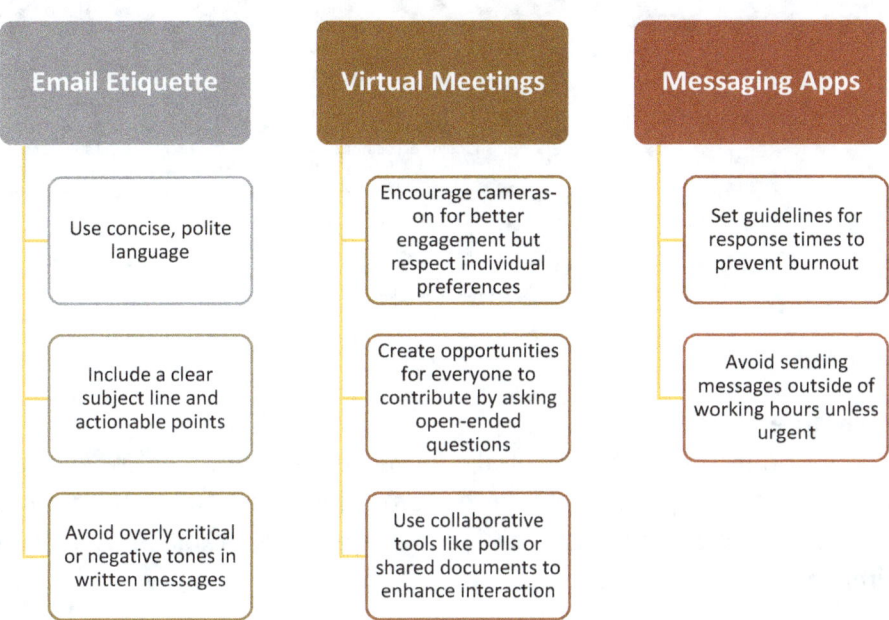

Example:
A Dubai-based advertising agency established a "No Messages After 6 PM" rule for its internal chat system, reducing employee stress and improving work-life balance.

Resolving Conflicts Through Communication

Conflicts are inevitable in any workplace, but they don't have to harm relationships or productivity. Effective communication can turn conflicts into opportunities for growth and collaboration.

Steps for Resolving Conflicts:

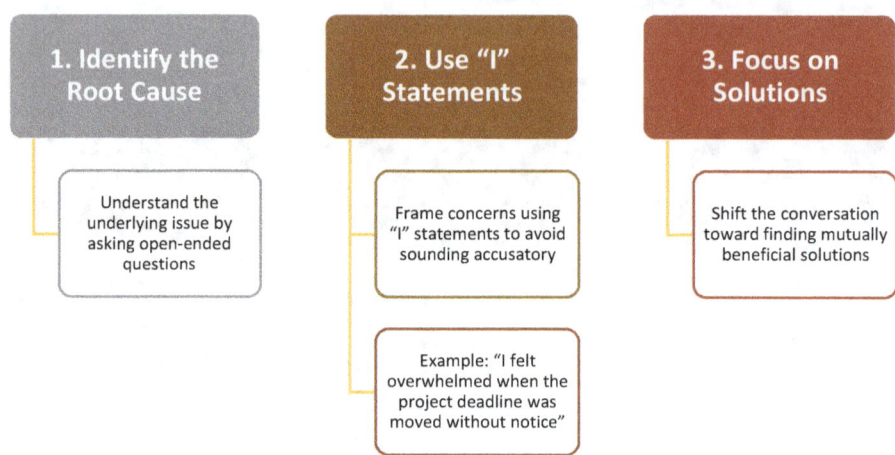

Example:
In a Bahrain-based hospital, a facilitated conflict resolution workshop equipped staff with communication tools to handle disagreements constructively. As a result, workplace harmony improved significantly.

Building a Culture of Communication

To sustain wellness through communication, organizations must embed open dialogue into their culture.

Organizational Strategies:

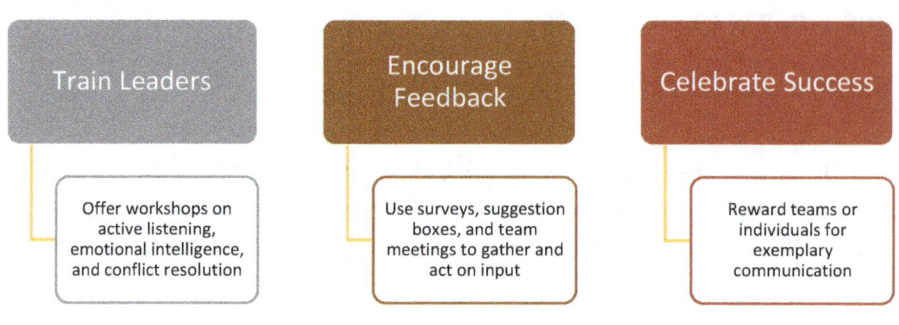

Example:
A financial institution in Qatar celebrated employees who exemplified excellent communication skills with monthly "Connector Awards," motivating others to improve their interactions.

Practical Exercises for Immediate Impact

Conclusion: Communication as a Wellness Tool

The way we communicate shapes the way we work. By prioritizing clear, empathetic, and effective communication, organizations can forward trust, reduce stress, and create environments where employees feel valued and connected.

Takeaway Challenge:

This week, focus on improving one aspect of your communication—whether it's practicing active listening, clarifying instructions, or delivering feedback thoughtfully. Notice how it enhances your interactions and contributes to workplace wellness.

3 BUILDING RESILIENCE IN THE WORKPLACE

Chapter 3: Building Resilience in the Workplace

Introduction: Turning Challenges into Opportunities

Resilience is the ability to recover, adapt, and thrive in the face of adversity. In a rapidly evolving workplace, resilience is no longer just a desirable trait—it's essential. Whether it's managing tight deadlines, navigating organizational changes, or handling personal challenges, resilience empowers employees and organizations to transform obstacles into opportunities.

This chapter explores how to cultivate resilience at both the individual and organizational levels, providing actionable strategies to build strength, adaptability, and optimism across your team.

The Pillars of Personal Resilience

1. Self-Awareness: Knowing Yourself to Strengthen Yourself

Resilience begins with self-awareness—the ability to recognize your stress triggers, strengths, and limits. Self-awareness equips individuals to take proactive steps to manage stress before it becomes overwhelming.

Example:
Sara, a marketing executive in Manama, discovered that looming deadlines increased her anxiety. By keeping a journal of her stress triggers, she identified patterns and implemented strategies like early task prioritization and mindfulness exercises. This simple practice turned her stress into a motivator for effective planning.

Practical Strategies:

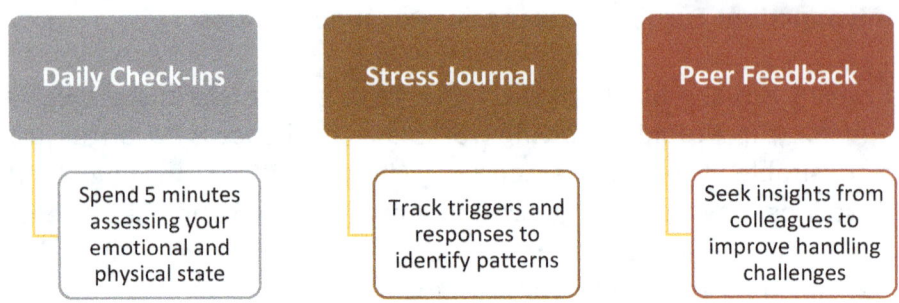

2. Mindset Shifts: Turning Setbacks into Setups for Success

A resilient mindset views challenges not as failures but as opportunities for growth. This perspective, often called a "growth mindset," promotes adaptability and optimism.

Example:
When Ali, a project manager in Riyadh, faced an unexpected project delay, he reframed it as an opportunity to refine his team's approach. By shifting the narrative, he turned frustration into motivation, resulting in a more efficient workflow.

Exercises to Practice Mindset Shifts:

- **Reframing Practice**: List three positive outcomes of a recent challenge to change your perspective.
- **Visualization**: Envision how overcoming current difficulties will contribute to future successes.

3. Physical and Emotional Well-Being: The Foundation of Resilience

Resilience is not just mental—it's deeply connected to physical health. Regular exercise, quality sleep, and proper nutrition enhance the body's ability to manage stress. Equally important is emotional well-being, which includes adopting positive relationships and managing emotions effectively.

Practical Actions:

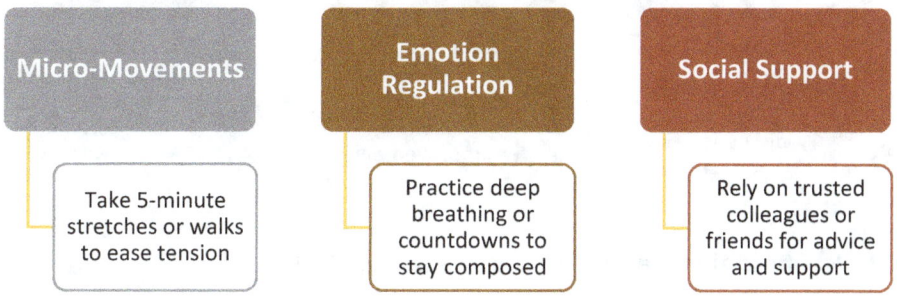

Building Resilient Teams: Strength in Unity

1. Collaborative Problem-Solving: Leveraging Collective Strengths

Resilient teams don't just survive adversity—they thrive by pooling diverse perspectives and skills to overcome obstacles.

Example:
A healthcare team in Bahrain faced a resource shortage during a high-demand period. By holding a brainstorming session, team members identified creative ways to redistribute workloads and streamline processes. Their collaborative approach not only resolved the issue but also strengthened team cohesion.

Tips for Building Collaborative Teams:

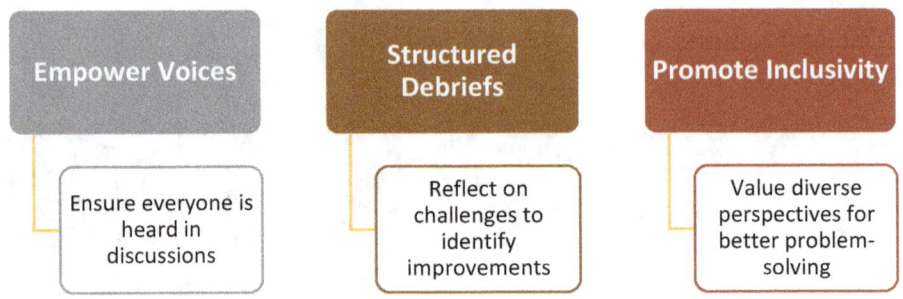

2. Psychological Safety: A Culture of Support

Teams thrive in environments where they feel safe to express ideas, admit mistakes, and seek help without fear of judgment. This "psychological safety" is a cornerstone of resilience.

Example:
In a Qatari financial firm, a team leader encouraged open dialogue by starting meetings with a "win or learn" segment. Team members shared successes and lessons from mistakes, encouraging trust and learning.

Steps to Build Psychological Safety:

Chapter 3: Building Resilience in the Workplace | 30

Organizational Resilience: Thriving Amid Change

1. Adaptive Leadership: Steering Through Uncertainty

Resilient organizations require leaders who can navigate uncertainty with clarity and confidence. Adaptive leaders guide their teams through change by remaining flexible, empathetic, and forward-thinking.

Example:
During a merger, a Kuwaiti oil company's CEO held weekly town halls to address employee concerns, share updates, and reinforce the organization's vision. This transparency reduced anxiety and promoted trust.

2. Proactive Policies: Preparing for the Unexpected

Organizations that anticipate and plan for challenges are better equipped to handle them. Proactive policies include crisis management plans, flexible work arrangements, and mental health resources.

Best Practices:

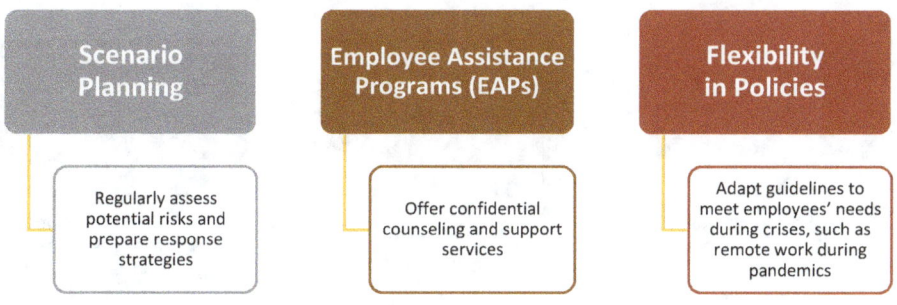

Real-Life Case Studies: Resilience in Action

Case Study 1: A Manufacturing Firm in Oman

Facing supply chain disruptions, the company empowered its logistics team to redesign delivery routes. By trusting their expertise and encouraging collaboration, the team minimized delays and restored client satisfaction.

Key Takeaway: Resilience grows when employees are given autonomy to solve problems.

Case Study 2: A Startup in Bahrain

To address high stress among developers, a tech startup introduced weekly mindfulness sessions and peer coaching programs. Within six months, team morale improved, and productivity increased by 15%.

Key Takeaway: Small, consistent wellness initiatives can have a significant impact.

Practical Tools for Resilience

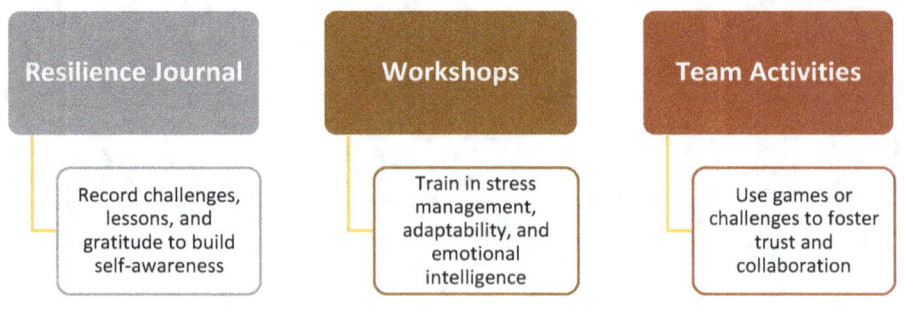

Conclusion: Resilience as a Superpower

Resilience is more than the ability to withstand adversity—it's the power to grow stronger through it. By promoting self-awareness, adopting a growth mindset, and building supportive teams, individuals and organizations can turn challenges into opportunities for transformation.

Takeaway Challenge:

This week, identify one resilience-building practice to integrate into your routine—whether it's journaling, mindfulness, or seeking feedback. Watch how this small change influences your perspective and energy.

Resilience isn't just a skill; it's a superpower. And when it becomes a shared value, it transforms workplaces into communities that thrive, no matter the challenge.

4. THE ROLE OF ROUTINE AND BOUNDARIES

Chapter 4: The Role of Routine and Boundaries

Introduction: Balancing Structure and Freedom

Imagine beginning your day with clarity and focus, knowing what to prioritize and when to step back. This balance, often elusive in today's demanding workplaces, is the essence of routines and boundaries. Far from being restrictive, they offer a framework for thriving—protecting energy, raising productivity, and nurturing well-being.

In this chapter, we'll explore how routines and boundaries serve as the foundation for mental and physical wellness. Through practical strategies, real-world examples, and actionable advice, we'll uncover how small, consistent actions can yield significant results and why healthy boundaries are indispensable for sustainable success.

The Power of Routines

Why Routines Matter

Routines reduce decision fatigue, create stability, and free mental bandwidth for innovation. By automating certain behaviors, they allow individuals to approach their day with greater focus and intention.

Example: In Manama, Layla, a team leader, starts her mornings with a 15-minute planning session. By visualizing her priorities, she avoids the midday slump and maintains her focus throughout the day.

Crafting Effective Routines

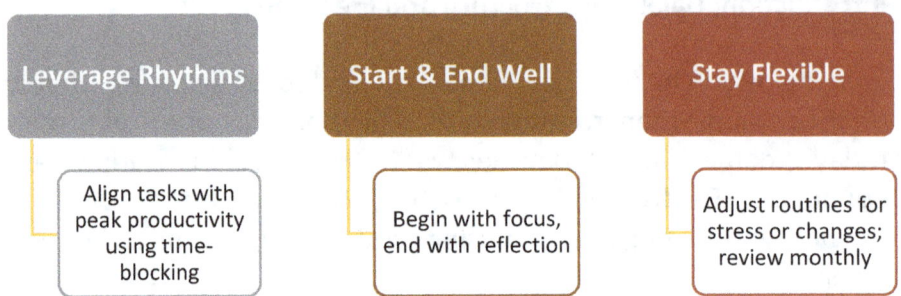

The Science of Taking Breaks

Why Breaks Are Essential

Breaks aren't a luxury—they're a necessity for sustaining focus and creativity. Research shows that stepping away, even briefly, helps prevent burnout and enhances problem-solving skills.

Example: A Bahrain-based IT firm implemented the Pomodoro Technique—25 minutes of focused work followed by a 5-minute break. The result? A **20% increase in task completion rates** and reduced employee fatigue.

Types of Breaks That Boost Wellness

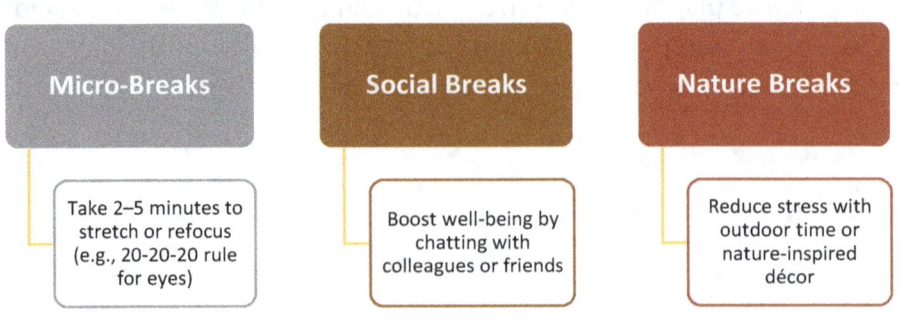

Setting Boundaries: Protecting Your Time and Energy

Physical Boundaries

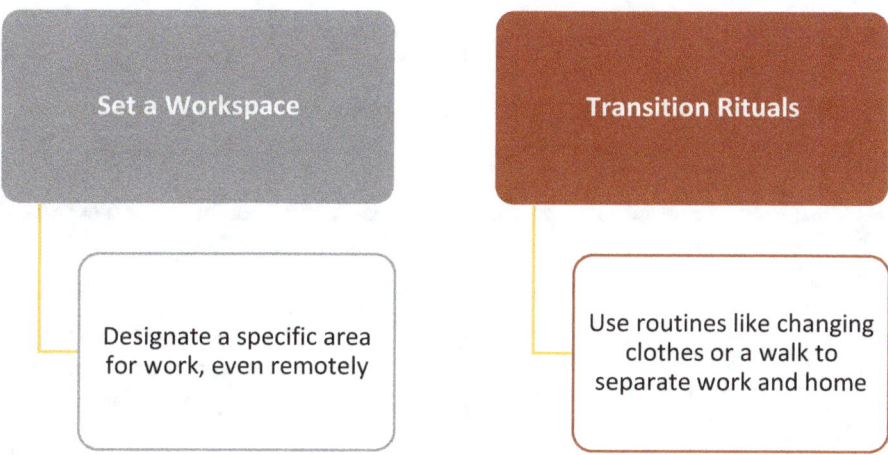

Temporal Boundaries

1. **Set Clear Working Hours**

   Communicate your availability to colleagues and stick to it. **Example**: Fatima, a remote worker in Riyadh, uses her calendar to signal her off-hours and protects her evenings for family time.

2. **Schedule Focus Time**

   Block uninterrupted work periods for deep tasks. **Pro Tip**: Label these blocks as "Meetings" to discourage interruptions.

Emotional Boundaries

Practice Saying No

Politely decline tasks that stretch you too thin

Pro Tip: Use phrases like, "I'd love to help, but I'm currently focused on [priority task]. Can we revisit this next week?"

Detox from Negativity

Limit interactions with energy-draining colleagues or activities

Exercise: Start and end your day by listing three things you're grateful for to maintain a positive outlook.

Technology: Friend or Foe?

Managing Digital Overload

Technology can either support productivity or become a source of distraction. It's crucial to manage its impact on mental clarity.

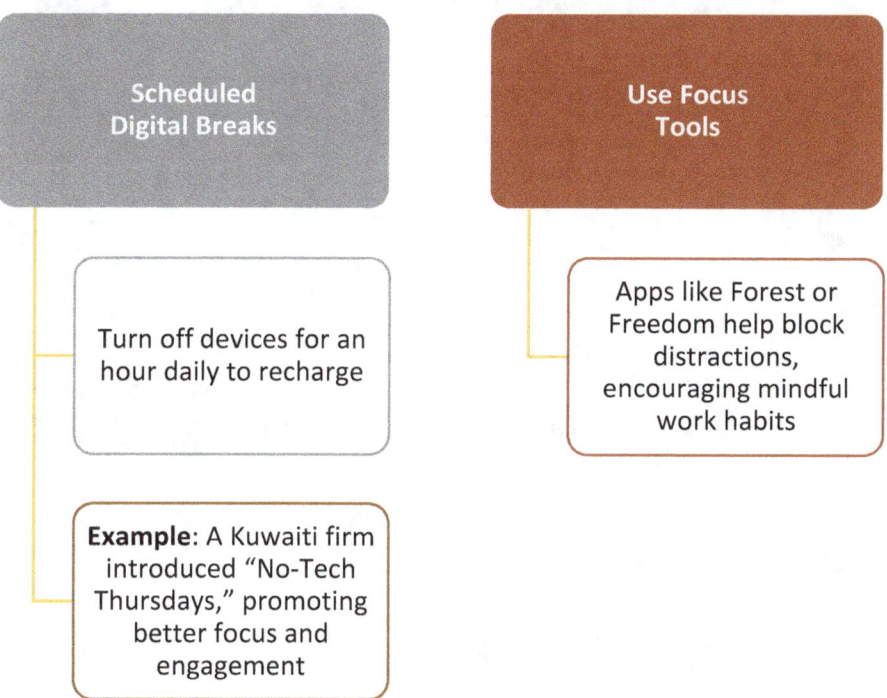

Creating a Workplace Culture That Respects Boundaries

Leadership's Role

Leaders play a critical role in modeling and respecting boundaries. **Example**: A Bahraini CEO set a company-wide rule against scheduling meetings after 4 PM, significantly improving work-life balance.

Policies That Promote Balance

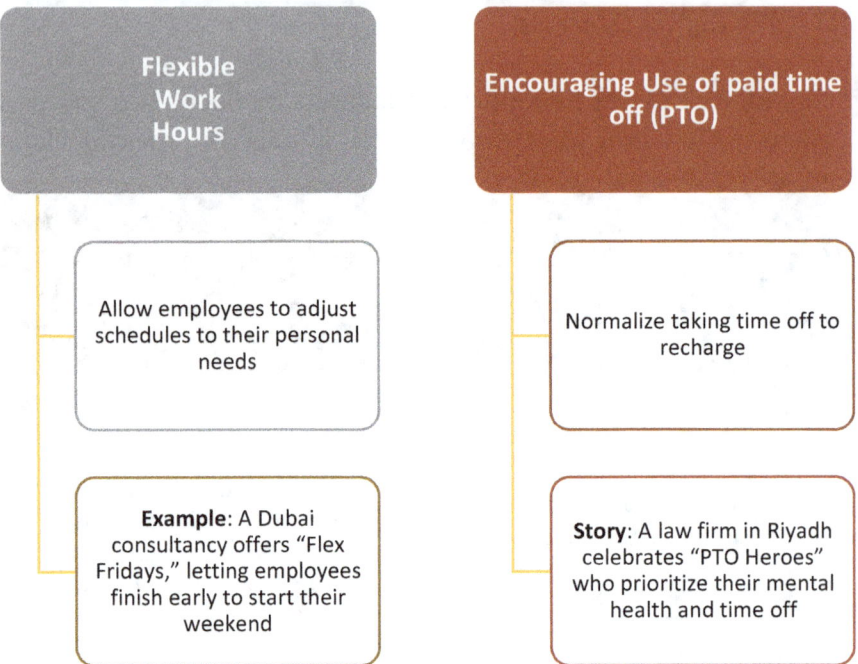

Real-Life Success Stories

1. **A Resilient Team in Qatar**

   Faced with tight deadlines, a construction company introduced "Wellness Wednesdays" featuring yoga and team lunches, resulting in reduced stress and higher productivity.

2. **Bahraini Healthcare Organization**

   After launching an education campaign on boundaries, staff reported a **35% improvement in work-life satisfaction** within six months.

Actionable Tips for Individuals and Teams

1. **Personal Reflection**

   Identify one area where your boundaries need reinforcement and take a small step to address it this week.

2. **Team Check-Ins**

   Dedicate the first 5 minutes of weekly meetings to discuss how well the team is balancing workloads.

3. **Accountability Buddies**

   Pair up with a colleague to keep each other accountable for sticking to routines and boundaries.

Conclusion: Routines and Boundaries as Wellness Anchors

Routines and boundaries aren't restrictive—they're liberating. They provide the structure to focus on what matters most while protecting your mental health.

Takeaway Challenge: Design one new routine and set one boundary this week. Whether it's starting your day with mindfulness or logging off emails at 6 PM, small steps can lead to lasting change.

5 CULTIVATING CONNECTION AND SUPPORT

Chapter 5: Cultivating Connection and Support

Introduction: The Power of Support and Connection

Think about a time when someone in your workplace made a difference simply by offering support. Maybe a colleague shared a piece of advice that guided you through a challenge, or a manager provided the encouragement you needed to push through a difficult project. These moments of connection are more than just feel-good experiences—they are the foundation of a thriving workplace.

In this chapter, we will explore how to cultivate authentic connections and support networks within your organization. We'll delve into mentorship, peer support, team collaboration, and building a culture that encourages the sharing of knowledge, experiences, and care. The goal is to create an environment where employees not only work together but truly support one another's growth and well-being.

The Importance of Connection and Support

Why Connection Matters

Human beings are social creatures by nature, and work is no different. Research consistently shows that employees who feel connected to their colleagues are more engaged, motivated, and committed to their work. When people feel supported, they are more likely to take risks, share innovative ideas, and collaborate openly.

Example:
At a large technology company in Bahrain, the introduction of "connectivity hours" (weekly designated times where employees meet informally over coffee) helped bridge communication gaps between departments. Employees felt more connected, and team collaboration skyrocketed, resulting in a 20% increase in efficiency.

The Benefits of Peer Support

A supportive work culture doesn't just make employees feel good; it has tangible business benefits. Peer support helps individuals cope with stress, manage their workload, and feel more confident in their roles. This, in turn, reduces burnout, enhances job satisfaction, and boosts overall performance.

Example:
A team at a finance company in Dubai struggled with stress during peak periods. They implemented a peer-support program where more experienced employees mentored new hires and those feeling overwhelmed. Not only did productivity improve, but the employees also reported higher morale and a greater sense of belonging.

Building Meaningful Mentorship Programs

The Role of Mentorship in Workplace Wellness

Mentorship is a powerful tool for both personal and professional growth. It provides employees with guidance, support, and a sense of direction, and it's one of the most effective ways to advance connection in the workplace. A strong mentorship program not only helps employees develop professionally but also provides them with emotional support, which can have lasting effects on their overall well-being.

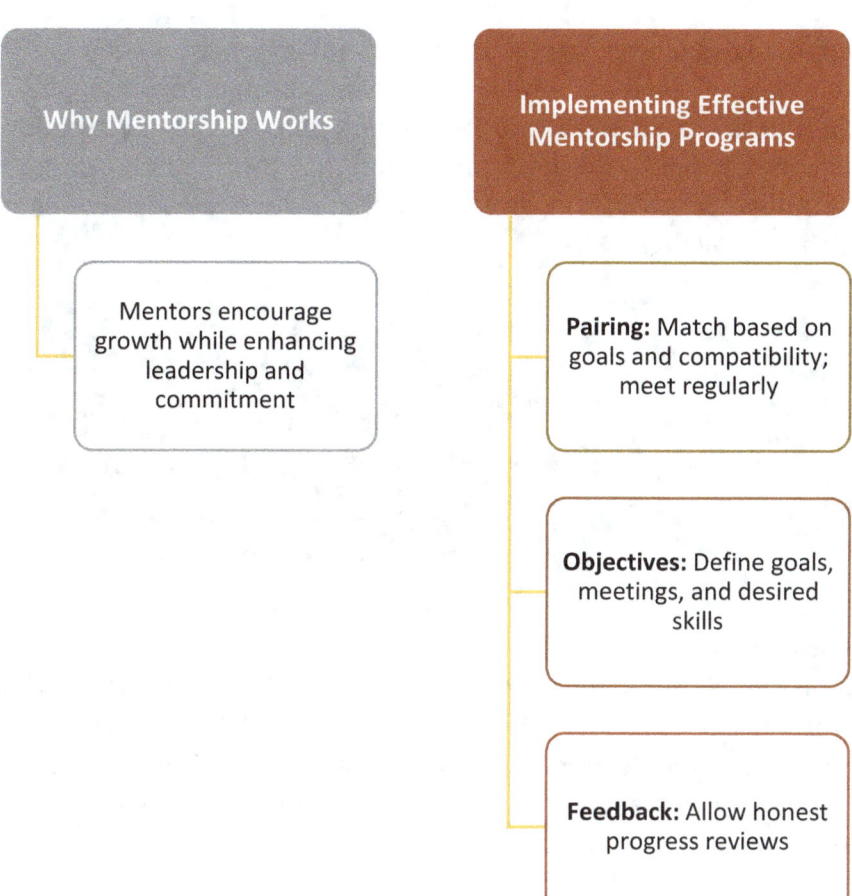

Example:

At a consultancy in Saudi Arabia, the implementation of a formal mentorship program with clear milestones led to a 35% increase in employee retention. Mentees reported feeling more confident in their roles and more connected to the organization.

Peer Support: Building Networks for Success

The Role of Peer Support in Mental Health

While mentorship provides formal guidance, peer support promotes an informal, yet equally crucial, system of care within teams. Peer support is especially important in maintaining mental health in the workplace. Colleagues who share similar roles and experiences are often better positioned to offer empathy and advice. By creating a culture of peer support, organizations can reduce isolation, encourage collaboration, and ensure that no one feels overwhelmed by their challenges.

Nurturing a Culture of Peer Support		
Open Conversations: Normalize discussions on mental health and stress	**Buddy Systems:** Pair employees to ease workplace navigation	**Wellness Initiatives:** Encourage regular check-ins, like "Wellness Wednesdays"

Example:
At a digital marketing firm in Doha, employees established an informal peer-support network through regular "wellness check-ins," where they would share their challenges, achievements, and tips for stress management. This initiative helped reduce burnout and boosted team cohesion.

Team Collaboration: Strengthening Workplace Bonds

Why Collaboration is Key

Collaboration is often viewed through the lens of productivity—how well teams can come together to complete projects and achieve goals. However, collaboration is just as important for wellness. When employees collaborate, they share knowledge, resources, and emotional support. A collaborative culture encourages inclusivity and reduces stress by allowing individuals to share responsibilities, lighten their workload, and feel part of a collective effort.

Team Collaboration		
Cross-Department Projects: Break silos, encourage shared purpose	**Digital Tools:** Use Slack, Asana, or Teams for efficient communication	**Team-Building:** Strengthen trust with activities like lunches or retreats

Example:

A real estate firm in Bahrain used cross-functional team projects to promote collaboration. By involving employees from marketing, sales, and customer service, they improved internal communication and reduced misunderstandings, leading to faster decision-making and better client relationships.

Creating a Supportive Work Culture

Leadership's Role in Cultivating Support

Leaders play an integral role in setting the tone for support within an organization. By modeling supportive behavior, actively listening to their team members, and creating policies that prioritize employee well-being, leaders nurture a culture of care that spreads through the entire organization.

Leading with Empathy:	
Be accessible, listen actively, and offer support.	Give growth-focused, constructive feedback.

Example:

A senior manager at a consulting firm in Dubai began offering weekly one-on-one sessions with his team members to check in on their well-being. The results were profound—employee satisfaction increased, and stress levels decreased, contributing to higher productivity.

Real-Life Examples of Success

Case Study: A Healthcare Team in Qatar

A hospital in Qatar introduced a mentorship program, peer support groups, and cross-functional collaboration workshops to tackle employee burnout and improve patient care. Within six months, employee satisfaction rates improved by **30%**, and patient care scores followed suit.

Case Study: A Tech Startup in Bahrain

This startup struggled with employee retention, especially among young professionals. By implementing a robust peer support system, team-building exercises, and a flexible work policy, turnover dropped by **25%** in the following year, and employee morale reached new heights.

Actionable Tips for Promoting Connection and Support

Conclusion: The Power of Connection

Building a culture of connection and support requires intentionality, time, and dedication. But the results—improved mental health,

Chapter 5: Cultivating Connection and Support | 48

stronger collaboration, and a more engaged workforce—are more than worth the effort. By prioritizing mentorship, peer support, and teamwork, you can create a workplace where employees feel cared for, valued, and motivated to succeed together.

Takeaway Challenge:

This week, reach out to a colleague, offer a word of encouragement, or introduce a new team-building activity. Small actions can lead to significant changes in your team's dynamics.

6 RECOGNITION AND VALIDATION

Chapter 6: Recognition and Validation

Introduction: The Transformative Power of Appreciation

Think about the last time someone genuinely acknowledged your efforts. How did it make you feel? Energized? Motivated? Valued? Recognition and validation are more than just niceties—they are the foundation of a thriving workplace. When employees feel recognized, they are more engaged, more productive, and more loyal to their organization. This is why recognition isn't just a bonus—it's a strategic tool for success.

Recognition is often seen as an afterthought, something we do when the job is done. But it should be embedded in every stage of work, from the daily grind to major achievements. When done right, recognition and validation can create an environment where people feel deeply connected to their work and the organization as a whole. In this chapter, we will explore the importance of recognition, the different types of recognition, and how organizations can adopt a culture of appreciation that drives long-term success.

Why Recognition Matters

The Power of Feeling Seen

At its core, recognition is about acknowledging the effort and value that individuals bring to their work. It's not just about rewarding success; it's about reinforcing behavior, validating effort, and showing people that their contributions matter. Recognition is a human need—it builds a sense of belonging, boosts self-esteem, and encourages people to continue to contribute meaningfully.

Research consistently shows that **employees who feel appreciated are more productive, more engaged, and more likely to stay with their employer**. According to Gallup, when employees are recognized for their work, they are more than **twice as likely to be**

engaged compared to those who are not. Moreover, they are **31% more likely to be productive**, leading to higher overall business performance.

Recognition also impacts mental health. When employees feel their efforts are seen and valued, stress levels decrease, and job satisfaction increases. Recognition is a tool for raising not only motivation but also **well-being**.

The Business Case for Recognition

Recognition isn't just a feel-good activity—it's directly linked to business success. Companies with a culture of recognition have lower turnover rates, higher employee satisfaction, and stronger performance metrics. When employees feel valued, they are more likely to go above and beyond, take ownership of their work, and collaborate more effectively with their peers.

For example, companies that prioritize employee recognition have **22% lower turnover** rates and **14% higher employee engagement**. This has a direct impact on the bottom line, with studies showing that employees who are engaged are **21% more profitable**.

Types of Recognition: More Than Just "Good Job!"

Recognition comes in many shapes and sizes. From small, informal gestures to formal, structured programs, every type of recognition serves a purpose. The key is to understand the different forms and use them appropriately.

1. Informal Recognition: The Power of Day-to-Day Appreciation

Small, everyday acts of recognition can have a huge impact on morale. A simple "thank you," a compliment during a meeting, or a handwritten note can go a long way in showing appreciation. These informal gestures are essential for creating an environment where recognition is a natural part of the work culture.

Example: Sarah, a project manager at a marketing agency, makes it a habit to start every meeting by thanking someone for their recent contribution, whether it's a successful campaign or a helpful gesture. This simple practice promotes a positive environment and encourages her team to keep giving their best.

2. Peer Recognition: Encouraging a Culture of Appreciation

Peer recognition is incredibly powerful because it comes from colleagues who understand the challenges and successes of the day-to-day work. When employees acknowledge each other's contributions, it builds fellowship, trust, and a sense of belonging.

Consider implementing peer recognition programs such as "Employee of the Month" or "Shout-Out Boards" where colleagues can publicly recognize one another. This not only boosts the morale of the individual being recognized but also promotes a culture of appreciation across the team.

In a study conducted by Gallup, 65% of employees said they would work harder if their efforts were recognized. Peer recognition often serves as a motivator for others, encouraging them to contribute positively as well.

3. Formal Recognition: Structured Programs that Reinforce Culture

While informal and peer recognition are essential, formal programs ensure that recognition is structured, consistent, and aligned with company values. These programs might include:

- **Employee of the Month** awards
- **Annual recognition programs** for long-term service or significant achievements

- **Bonuses** or **gift vouchers** for outstanding performance
- **Public recognition** at company-wide meetings or events

These programs are essential for reinforcing desired behaviors and motivating employees to reach for excellence.

The Role of Leaders in Recognition

Leaders play a crucial role in the recognition process. When leaders recognize their employees, they set the tone for the entire organization. If leadership neglects recognition, it can send the message that hard work is undervalued, leading to disengagement and a lack of motivation. On the other hand, when leaders consistently recognize and reward contributions, they create an environment of trust, respect, and motivation.

1. Lead by Example

Leaders should model recognition by acknowledging the efforts of their teams regularly. When leaders express gratitude and appreciation, it demonstrates the value placed on employees, which trickles down to the rest of the organization. Furthermore, public recognition of employees by leaders sends a message that hard work is not only appreciated but celebrated.

Example: A CEO in a Saudi Arabian company made it a point to personally thank employees for their contributions, especially when facing difficult tasks. This public display of recognition helped solidify the company's reputation as a great place to work, improving employee satisfaction and retention.

2. Be Specific in Your Praise

It's not enough to say "good job." Be specific about what the employee did and how it impacted the team or organization. Specificity shows that you are paying attention and that their efforts have made a difference. This adds weight to the recognition and makes it more meaningful.

Example: Instead of a generic "Good work on the presentation," say, "Your ability to distill complex information and present it so clearly was incredibly valuable. It made a huge difference in how the client understood our proposal."

Overcoming Recognition Challenges

While recognition is a powerful tool, implementing it effectively can come with challenges. Let's explore some common obstacles and how to overcome them.

1. Avoiding Favoritism

One of the biggest pitfalls in recognition programs is favoritism. When some employees are consistently recognized while others are overlooked, it can breed resentment and disengagement. To combat this, make recognition a regular and inclusive practice, ensuring that everyone's contributions are acknowledged.

Solution: Create clear criteria for recognition that focus on behavior and results, not just personal preferences. Rotating recognition programs and providing opportunities for different team members to be celebrated ensures fairness.

2. Ensuring Consistency

Recognition can lose its impact if it's inconsistent. If employees only hear "thank you" during annual reviews or major achievements, it becomes less meaningful.

Solution: Build recognition into your day-to-day practices. This can be as simple as taking a moment during meetings to acknowledge someone's contributions or using team communications to celebrate small wins.

3. Keeping Recognition Aligned with Company Values

For recognition to be effective, it must align with the organization's core values. Recognizing the wrong behavior can send mixed messages and may not have the desired impact.

Solution: Ensure that recognition programs highlight behaviors and values that reflect the company's mission. Rewarding collaboration, innovation, or customer-centric efforts reinforces the culture you want to cultivate.

Creating a Culture of Recognition

Building a culture of recognition requires intentionality, consistency, and effort. It's not just about having a recognition program in place; it's about integrating appreciation into the company's core practices. To create a culture where recognition thrives, consider these steps:

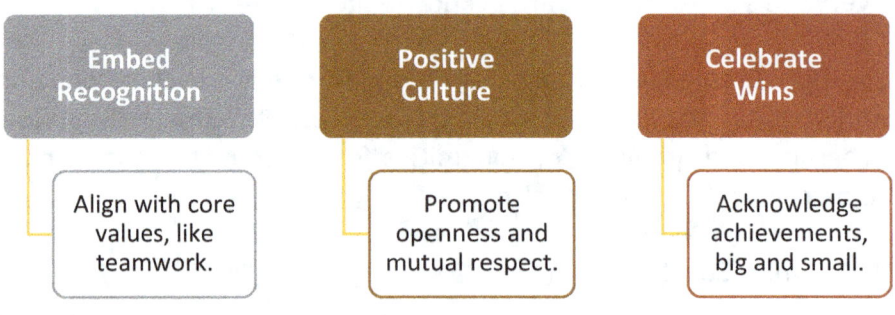

Conclusion: The Lasting Impact of Recognition

Recognition and validation are not just about offering praise; they are about creating an environment where employees feel genuinely appreciated, valued, and motivated. By embedding recognition into your organizational culture, you'll raise engagement, enhance morale, and improve overall business outcomes. A workplace where employees are seen and appreciated is one where people thrive—and where organizations succeed.

Takeaway Challenge: This week, make a conscious effort to recognize at least one colleague or team member for their contribution. Be specific in your praise and make it meaningful. Watch as this simple act of appreciation elevates their mood, their work, and their connection to the organization.

7 WELLNESS-FOCUSED POLICIES AND BENEFITS

Chapter 7: Wellness-Focused Policies and Benefits

Introduction: Turning Wellness Into a Strategic Advantage

In today's fast-paced, competitive world, employee wellness is no longer a luxury or an afterthought—it's a strategic imperative. Organizations that prioritize wellness initiatives not only benefit from improved employee well-being but also see tangible gains in productivity, morale, and retention. Creating wellness-focused policies and benefits is about more than offering perks; it's about building a supportive and sustainable framework that enables your employees to thrive.

In this chapter, we'll explore how to design, implement, and measure wellness policies that promotes a culture of care and high performance. From physical health to mental well-being and financial stability, wellness policies play a key role in shaping an organization's culture and long-term success.

Why Wellness-Focused Policies Matter

The Business Case for Wellness Policies

Organizations that invest in wellness-focused policies see far-reaching benefits that go beyond just employee happiness. Research consistently shows that wellness programs lead to:

- **Increased productivity**: When employees feel supported and well, they're more engaged and motivated.
- **Higher retention rates**: Employees are more likely to stay with a company that cares about their health and well-being.
- **Lower healthcare costs**: Proactive wellness programs reduce the frequency and severity of workplace injuries, illnesses, and mental health issues.

Beyond these measurable benefits, wellness policies also enhance an organization's **brand reputation**. In a world where corporate responsibility is valued by consumers and potential employees alike, organizations that prioritize wellness stand out as employers of choice.

Example: A global consulting firm introduced comprehensive mental health support programs, including confidential counseling and wellness apps. Over the next year, they saw a **15% improvement in employee retention** and a **30% reduction in absenteeism**.

The Human Impact of Wellness Policies

Wellness-focused policies directly affect the individuals who make up your workforce. They create environments where employees feel physically energized, emotionally supported, and mentally resilient. A thriving workforce isn't just good for business—it's good for the community, creating positive ripple effects that extend beyond the office.

Employees who have access to wellness programs are **less stressed**, **more engaged**, and ultimately, **more satisfied** with their jobs. This emotional and physical well-being enhances overall performance, collaboration, and morale. When employees feel taken care of, they're more likely to take pride in their work and contribute to the organization's mission.

Designing Effective Wellness Policies

Step 1: Understand the Needs of Your Employees

Before implementing any wellness initiative, it's crucial to understand your employees' specific needs and challenges. Every workforce is unique, so a one-size-fits-all approach won't work.

Conduct Employee Surveys	Host Focus Groups
Use surveys or feedback forms to identify employees' wellness needs, such as stress management or flexible working hours	Conduct focus groups with employees from diverse departments to uncover wellness insights beyond surveys

Example: After conducting a series of surveys, a tech firm in Dubai discovered that many of its employees were struggling with work-life balance due to long working hours. In response, the company introduced flexible scheduling and remote working options, leading to **a 25% increase in employee satisfaction**.

Step 2: Create a Comprehensive Wellness Framework

A truly effective wellness policy addresses multiple aspects of well-being—physical health, mental health, financial wellness, and social support. Let's break these down:

1. **Physical Health Policies**:
    - Offer access to gym memberships or wellness apps.
    - Encourage regular health screenings or flu vaccinations.
    - Provide ergonomically designed workstations to prevent physical strain.

Example: A manufacturing company in Bahrain introduced on-site fitness classes and free gym memberships for employees. As a result, employee engagement increased by **18%**, and absenteeism decreased due to fewer health-related sick days.

2. **Mental Health Support**:
    - Provide confidential counseling services.
    - Implement mental health days as part of paid time off (PTO).
    - Offer workshops on stress management, resilience, and mindfulness.
3. **Financial Wellness**:
    - Provide access to financial counseling services.
    - Offer retirement savings plans or matching contributions.
    - Educate employees on budgeting, saving, and managing debt through workshops or partnerships with financial advisors.

Example: A financial services firm in Saudi Arabia introduced a financial wellness program that included savings matching, budgeting classes, and debt management workshops. Within six months, employees reported feeling **30% more confident** about their financial security.

4. **Social and Community Support**:
    - Promote a sense of belonging through social events, team-building activities, or volunteer opportunities.
    - Create spaces for employees to connect, like social lounges or virtual meetups.

Implementing Wellness Policies Successfully

Step 1: Communicate Clearly and Consistently

To ensure the success of your wellness initiatives, clear and consistent communication is key. Employees must be aware of the programs available to them and understand how to access them.

1. **Create a Wellness Hub**: Develop an easily accessible wellness portal on your company's intranet or website where

employees can find information about available benefits, programs, and upcoming wellness events.
2. **Host Wellness Kickoff Events**: Launch new wellness programs with an event or webinar that explains the offerings and how employees can get involved.

Example: A government agency in Qatar introduced a wellness portal that employees could access 24/7 for resources on mental health, fitness programs, and financial planning. As a result, **program engagement increased by 40%** in the first quarter.

Step 2: Encourage Participation and Engagement

It's important to incentivize participation in wellness programs and ensure employees feel motivated to get involved.

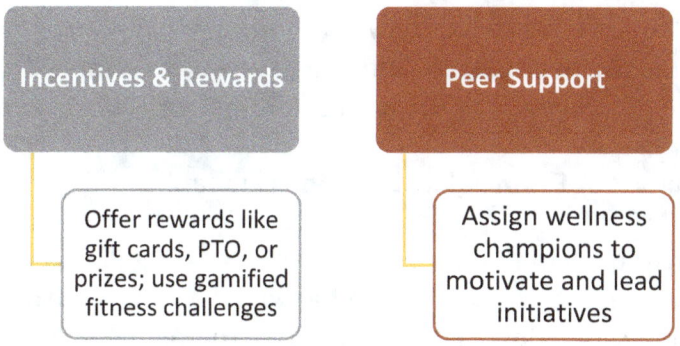

Overcoming Common Wellness Challenges

While wellness policies can significantly improve employee well-being, there are common barriers to success. Here's how to overcome them:

Real-Life Case Studies

Case Study 1: A Healthcare Organization in Bahrain

A hospital in Bahrain struggled with high burnout rates among its nursing staff. In response, they implemented a wellness program that included stress reduction workshops, peer support groups, and regular mental health days. Within a year, burnout rates dropped by **30%**, and employee satisfaction rose dramatically.

Case Study 2: A Financial Institution in Dubai

This firm noticed that many employees were struggling with financial stress, which affected productivity. They introduced a comprehensive financial wellness program, including debt management tools, retirement planning workshops, and one-on-one financial coaching. Employees reported a **40% decrease in financial anxiety**, and workplace morale improved.

Conclusion: Making Wellness a Long-Term Investment

Creating wellness-focused policies and benefits is an investment that pays dividends not just in employee well-being, but in business success. By prioritizing wellness in the workplace, you are promoting a culture of care, trust, and productivity that benefits everyone.

With clear communication, thoughtful design, and a commitment to measurement, you can build a thriving, resilient workforce that is ready to take on the challenges of today and tomorrow.

8 LEADERSHIP'S ROLE IN WELLNESS

Chapter 8: Leadership's Role in Wellness

Introduction: The Foundation of a Wellness-Centered Culture

When it comes to building a culture of wellness in the workplace, the most important factor is leadership. Leaders not only define the strategic direction of the organization but also set the tone for its culture. If wellness is to become a foundational element of the organization, leaders must prioritize it, model it, and continuously advocate for it. Leadership is about much more than delegating tasks and meeting targets—it's about creating an environment where employees can flourish, feel supported, and thrive both professionally and personally.

In this chapter, we will explore the profound impact leadership has on workplace wellness, how leaders can integrate wellness into their leadership style, and the transformative role they play in cultivating a wellness-centered organizational culture.

Leadership as a Catalyst for Wellness

Leading by Example: The Power of Modeling Wellness

Effective leadership in wellness begins with the leader. Leaders are the role models who demonstrate the behaviors they want to see throughout the organization. When leaders take wellness seriously—by prioritizing their own well-being, encouraging healthy work-life balance, and openly discussing mental health—they signal to employees that wellness is important and worth investing in.

Example:
A CEO in Dubai publicly shared his experience of managing stress through regular mindfulness sessions. His openness inspired his leadership team to adopt similar practices, and soon, mindfulness became a core part of the company's culture, with employees across departments participating in sessions. This approach didn't just

improve the employees' mental health; it also raised a more inclusive, empathetic workplace where everyone felt empowered to prioritize their well-being.

The Role of Vulnerability in Leadership

Leaders who show vulnerability can connect with their teams on a deeper level. This doesn't mean compromising professionalism, but rather acknowledging that they, too, face challenges and have personal struggles. Vulnerability nurtures a sense of trust and empathy within teams, which is critical to establishing a culture of wellness.

When leaders openly acknowledge their own stress, anxiety, or burnout, they humanize themselves. It creates space for employees to do the same. This transparency eliminates stigma and encourages employees to be proactive about their mental health.

Example:
A senior manager in a Bahrain-based consultancy shared her experience of burnout during a team meeting, explaining the steps she took to address it and inviting others to talk openly about their challenges. This created a safe environment where employees were more willing to speak up and seek support.

Leadership Behaviors That Promote Wellness

1. Prioritizing Well-Being in Decision-Making

Leaders must ensure that well-being is considered in every decision they make. Whether it's adopting flexible working arrangements, providing mental health resources, or ensuring work-life balance, every decision should reflect the organization's commitment to employee health and wellness.

For example, when faced with tight deadlines, leaders can consider how to best distribute the workload to avoid overwhelming employees, recognizing that long hours are not sustainable in the long run. Likewise, leaders can offer employees the flexibility to adjust their schedules when personal matters arise.

Example:
A leader in a Qatari financial institution noticed an increase in burnout symptoms among employees due to constant overtime. In response, she implemented flexible scheduling and encouraged employees to take "mental health days" when necessary. This resulted in increased productivity and job satisfaction, as employees felt their health and well-being were valued.

2. Establishing Clear Wellness Policies

Leaders should ensure wellness is woven into the company's policies and daily practices. These policies should include provisions for mental health, flexible working arrangements, time-off policies, and access to wellness resources. Leaders must not only champion these policies but also make sure they are integrated into the company's day-to-day operations.

Example:
At a manufacturing company in Kuwait, the leadership team introduced an initiative where managers were trained to recognize signs of burnout and stress in employees. They also provided clear guidelines on how employees could access counseling services and mental health support. This proactive approach resulted in a noticeable decrease in stress-related absenteeism and a more open culture regarding mental health.

3. Celebrating and Rewarding Wellness Efforts

Leaders play a key role in recognizing and rewarding efforts to prioritize wellness. By celebrating employees who model healthy behaviors—whether it's attending a wellness workshop, taking the initiative in promoting work-life balance, or organizing stress-relief activities—leaders reinforce the importance of these behaviors and encourage others to follow suit.

Example:
A Saudi Arabia-based consulting firm regularly celebrates employees who participate in wellness challenges or take steps to improve their health, such as achieving fitness milestones or attending wellness workshops. This public recognition not only boosts morale but also promotes a culture of wellness, where employees are encouraged to take an active role in their own well-being.

Building a Wellness-Centered Organization: Leadership's Strategic Role

1. Integrating Wellness into Organizational Goals

The commitment to wellness should be reflected in the organization's strategic goals. Wellness should not be seen as a "nice-to-have" but as an integral part of the organization's long-term success. Leaders should actively incorporate wellness into the company's values, vision, and mission statement. This alignment ensures that wellness is embedded in the organization's DNA.

Example:
In a forward-thinking technology company in Dubai, wellness was made a central part of their organizational vision, with the CEO directly linking employee well-being to the company's success in their mission statement. This alignment helped promote a deep commitment to wellness initiatives across all levels of the organization.

2. Creating a Culture of Support and Openness

Leaders should create an environment where employees feel safe discussing their well-being and health needs. Creating such a culture requires consistent efforts from leadership, including setting expectations for respect, openness, and support. Employees should feel comfortable sharing their challenges and seeking help without fear of stigma or judgment.

Example:
A hospital in Bahrain implemented a monthly wellness roundtable where leaders and employees could openly discuss mental health challenges, share coping strategies, and discuss how wellness programs could be improved. This helped create a more empathetic and supportive workplace, where wellness was seen as a shared priority.

The Long-Term Impact of Leadership in Wellness

Leaders who embrace wellness and promote it authentically will ultimately cultivate a resilient workforce. A wellness-centered leadership approach will not only lead to healthier employees but will also inspire loyalty, increase job satisfaction, and improve organizational performance.

By promoting wellness as an ongoing, integral part of the organization, leaders can contribute to building an environment where employees feel not just supported but empowered. This empowerment, in turn, drives innovation, collaboration, and business success.

Conclusion: The Leadership Imperative

Leadership in wellness is not just a role—it's a responsibility. By setting the right example, integrating wellness into the organization's culture, and creating policies that support well-being, leaders have the power to transform the workplace into a space where employees can thrive.

The path to a wellness-centered organization starts with leadership—and with every small step you take, you'll create an environment where employees aren't just working; they are flourishing.

Takeaway Challenge:

This week, take one action to prioritize wellness in your leadership approach. Whether it's setting boundaries for work hours, offering flexible schedules, or simply checking in with a team member about their well-being, your leadership can make a lasting impact on your team's health and success.

9 MEASURING AND SUSTAINING WELLNESS

Chapter 9: Measuring and Sustaining Wellness

Introduction: The Journey of Wellness—Tracking Progress and Ensuring Longevity

Wellness in the workplace is a journey—not a destination. While launching wellness programs and initiatives is crucial, it is the sustained effort, regular monitoring, and adaptability that ensures their success. Creating a workplace where wellness is prioritized involves measuring the impact of initiatives, adapting based on data, and building a culture where wellness continues to thrive over time.

In this chapter, we'll explore how to measure the effectiveness of your wellness programs, identify the necessary metrics, and ensure that wellness remains an enduring part of your workplace culture.

Why Measuring Wellness Matters

The Importance of Tracking Progress

Measuring wellness initiatives is not only about proving their effectiveness; it's also about understanding how they evolve over time. When you actively measure the impact of wellness programs, you can identify areas of improvement, recognize what works, and fine-tune strategies to address emerging needs.

Without measurement, wellness initiatives risk becoming irrelevant or disconnected from the organization's goals. Tracking wellness helps ensure that programs are truly benefiting employees and contributing to a positive work environment.

Example:
A Dubai-based company launched a wellness initiative offering mental health days and flexible working hours. By tracking participation rates and employee satisfaction through surveys, they identified that employees were most engaged with the mental

health days. As a result, they increased the allocation of mental health days and saw a **25% increase in employee engagement** and a significant reduction in burnout levels.

Key Metrics to Track Wellness Success

1. Participation Rates

One of the most straightforward ways to measure wellness success is through participation rates. How many employees are engaging with the wellness programs? Participation indicates interest and suggests that the programs are meeting the needs of employees.

Example:
A tech company in Bahrain offered weekly mindfulness sessions and tracked how many employees attended. Within six months, attendance grew by **40%**, indicating that employees were not only interested in the programs but also found value in them.

Tracking participation rates helps identify popular programs, but also areas where interest may be low, allowing for refinements or replacements.

2. Employee Satisfaction

Measuring satisfaction is key to understanding the perceived value of wellness programs. Are employees satisfied with the resources available to them? Are they experiencing benefits from the programs offered?

Tools for Measurement:

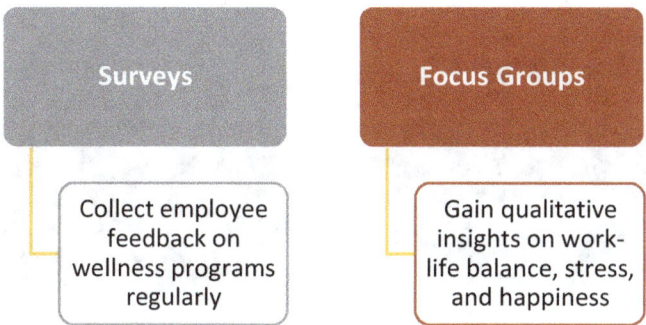

Example:
A financial institution in Qatar regularly surveyed employees about the mental health support services offered. Feedback showed that employees felt more supported, and satisfaction rates rose by **30%** in just a year, demonstrating the positive impact of wellness offerings.

3. Absenteeism and Turnover Rates

Tracking absenteeism and turnover rates provides valuable insight into how wellness programs impact employee well-being. High rates of absenteeism or turnover may indicate that wellness initiatives aren't addressing the underlying issues employees are facing.

Example:
After a manufacturing firm in Oman introduced flexible working hours and stress management workshops, absenteeism decreased by **15%**, and employee turnover dropped by **20%** over the course of a year. These numbers demonstrated that the wellness initiatives helped reduce stress and contributed to greater work-life balance.

4. Productivity and Performance Metrics

While wellness programs focus on improving well-being, they also have a direct impact on employee performance. Healthier, happier employees are more likely to be productive and engaged in their work.

Tools for Measurement:

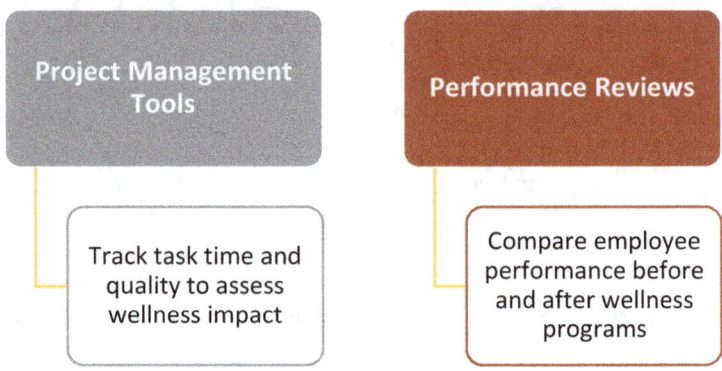

Example:
A healthcare organization in Bahrain integrated a wellness program that included physical fitness challenges and mindfulness workshops. After six months, the company noted a **20% improvement in project completion times** and a noticeable reduction in workplace conflicts.

Tools and Methods for Measuring Wellness Impact

1. Wellness Dashboards

A wellness dashboard centralizes key data points, giving you a clear, visual overview of wellness program performance. These dashboards can track participation rates, satisfaction scores, absenteeism, and other key metrics, offering real-time insights.

Example:
A leading construction firm in Kuwait implemented a wellness dashboard that tracked employee health participation, wellness days used, and productivity metrics. This tool allowed the company to identify trends, such as a spike in wellness days following

particularly intense work periods, prompting them to introduce additional support during those times.

2. Pulse Surveys and Feedback Loops

Continuous feedback is essential to the ongoing success of wellness programs. Pulse surveys, which are short and frequent surveys, allow you to gather feedback quickly and adapt swiftly to any issues employees may be facing.

Example:
A marketing agency in Dubai began conducting monthly pulse surveys to assess employee stress levels and satisfaction with their wellness programs. The feedback led to adjustments, such as introducing more flexible scheduling options, which ultimately improved employee engagement and productivity.

Ensuring Wellness Programs Remain Sustainable

1. Regular Program Evaluation

Wellness programs need regular evaluation to ensure they remain relevant and impactful. These evaluations should be based on both qualitative and quantitative data, allowing you to make informed decisions about future initiatives.

Example:
A telecom company in Saudi Arabia conducts an annual review of its wellness initiatives, including focus groups, surveys, and data analysis. This evaluation led to the introduction of new initiatives, such as financial wellness workshops, in response to employee feedback about financial stress.

2. Adapting Programs to Meet Changing Needs

Employees' wellness needs will evolve over time. What works today may not be as effective tomorrow. For example, if a global pandemic or economic downturn occurs, employees may need different types of support.

To keep wellness programs relevant, regularly adapt them based on ongoing employee feedback, market trends, and organizational needs.

Example:
A global company in Bahrain initially offered fitness challenges and healthy eating programs. As remote work became the norm, they adapted by introducing virtual wellness workshops, stress-relief techniques, and online fitness classes, which kept employees engaged and supported.

3. Leadership Commitment to Wellness

For wellness programs to succeed long-term, leadership must actively support them. Leaders should consistently reinforce the importance of wellness and lead by example. Their engagement in wellness initiatives makes it clear to employees that wellness is a priority.

Example:
A leader in a Riyadh-based software company regularly participates in wellness activities, from virtual mindfulness sessions to fitness challenges. This leadership engagement has encouraged others to join, creating a culture of wellness that permeates the organization.

The Challenges in Measuring Wellness

1. Low Engagement or Participation

Sometimes, programs experience low engagement. This can be due to a lack of awareness, inadequate promotion, or a disconnect between the wellness offerings and employees' actual needs.

Solution:
Regular communication and employee involvement in the design process can help increase engagement. Tailor programs based on employee preferences and feedback to improve participation.

2. Limited Resources

Many organizations struggle with resource constraints, especially when it comes to budgeting for wellness initiatives.

Solution:
Start with small, cost-effective initiatives that can scale over time. Many wellness programs, such as mental health support groups or fitness challenges, require little financial investment but can yield substantial benefits.

Real-Life Success Stories

Case Study 1: A Manufacturing Firm in Bahrain

Challenge: High stress levels and high turnover.

Solution:

- Introduced mindfulness workshops, flexible working hours, and regular wellness check-ins.
- Measured success using employee satisfaction surveys and tracking absenteeism and turnover rates.

Results:

- Turnover decreased by **20%**, absenteeism dropped by **15%**, and employee satisfaction increased significantly.

Case Study 2: A Tech Firm in Dubai

Challenge: Low participation in existing wellness programs.

Solution:

- Conducted pulse surveys to gather feedback from employees.
- Introduced virtual wellness programs, including mental health webinars and fitness challenges.

Results:

- Employee participation in wellness programs increased by **45%**.
- Productivity improved by **20%**, with employees reporting feeling more engaged and energized.

Practical Tips for Measuring and Sustaining Wellness

1. **Build a Wellness Team**

   Create a team responsible for gathering data, reviewing progress, and making recommendations for improvements.

2. **Conduct Quarterly Wellness Audits**

   Evaluate the effectiveness of programs at least once every quarter. Adapt initiatives based on data and feedback.

3. **Celebrate Wellness Achievements**

Acknowledge milestones, such as the percentage of employees participating or improvements in wellness metrics, to motivate continued engagement.

Conclusion: Wellness is a Continuous Journey

Measuring and sustaining wellness programs ensures their long-term success and impact. By using data, adapting to changing needs, and making wellness a priority, organizations can create an environment where employees thrive, innovate, and stay engaged.

Takeaway Challenge:

This week, evaluate the current wellness programs in your organization. Collect feedback, assess engagement levels, and identify one area for improvement. By doing so, you'll ensure that wellness remains a continuous journey for everyone involved.

CONCLUSION: A CALL TO ACTION FOR WELLNESS

Conclusion: A Call to Action for Wellness

As we reach the end of this journey, take a moment to imagine the workplace of the future: a place where employees feel empowered, supported, and genuinely valued. A place where wellness isn't an afterthought or a fleeting initiative, but a deeply ingrained part of the organization's fabric. This workplace isn't a distant dream—it's within our reach. By integrating wellness into our everyday practices, we can transform workplaces into spaces where people don't just work, but **thrive**.

Workplace wellness is not merely about implementing programs or policies; it's about creating a **sustainable culture** where every individual feels seen, heard, and cared for. It's about nurturing an environment that recognizes the whole person—body, mind, and spirit. The truth is that when employees feel supported in all aspects of their well-being, they not only perform better, but they feel more **connected** and **fulfilled** in their roles. And this, in turn, leads to greater organizational success.

Throughout this book, we have explored the many facets of wellness—from leadership's pivotal role in setting the tone to building meaningful connections, from creating policies that empower employees to ensuring sustainability through measurement and adaptation. Now, it's time to take action. This is your call to turn these principles into practices that will benefit not only your teams but also your entire organization.

Reflecting on What We've Learned

As we wrap up the journey, let's revisit the key insights that we've explored in this book, each of which contributes to the foundation of a successful wellness strategy:

1. **Leadership Sets the Tone**

   Leaders are the catalysts for creating a culture of wellness. When leaders prioritize their own well-being and model balanced behaviors, they send a clear message to their teams: wellness matters. Leadership's commitment is essential for embedding wellness into the DNA of an organization, making it a part of everyday practice rather than a temporary initiative.

2. **The Power of Connection**

   Workplace wellness thrives when employees feel connected—whether through mentorship, peer support, or collaborative teams. Strong relationships build trust, improves communication, and create a sense of belonging, which directly impacts mental health and engagement.

3. **Comprehensive Policies Empower Employees**

   Wellness-focused policies address not only physical health but also emotional and mental well-being. By offering flexible hours, mental health days, and wellness programs, organizations can help employees manage stress, balance personal responsibilities, and find fulfillment in their work.

4. **Sustainability and Adaptation Are Key**

   Wellness is not a one-off project—it's a continuous journey. By regularly measuring the impact of wellness initiatives and adapting them to meet evolving needs, organizations can ensure long-term success and maintain engagement. Continuous evaluation and feedback loops allow wellness programs to stay relevant, effective, and impactful.

5. **The Ripple Effect of Wellness**

   The benefits of wellness extend beyond the workplace, influencing families, communities, and society as a whole. By investing in your employees' well-being, you're helping to create a ripple effect that improves lives inside and outside the office. Healthy employees create healthy families, and healthy families create thriving communities.

A Global Perspective: Wellness as a Movement

The trend toward workplace wellness is not just a local phenomenon—it's a global movement. From tech hubs in Silicon Valley to innovative firms in the Middle East, organizations worldwide are embracing wellness as a cornerstone of their culture. For instance, **friluftsliv** (open-air living), a wellness philosophy popular in Scandinavia, encourages outdoor meetings and connection with nature. Similarly, in the Gulf region, companies are integrating flexible working hours and mindfulness practices to support mental health.

This growing global shift emphasizes that wellness is no longer a "nice-to-have" perk, but a critical element in advancing healthy, engaged, and productive teams. As we move forward, we must embrace this cultural change and make wellness a priority in every organization, regardless of size or sector.

A Call for Collaboration Across Roles

Wellness cannot be achieved by one person or department alone; it requires a collective effort. Leaders, HR teams, and employees must work together to create a supportive, wellness-centered environment. Leaders provide the vision and model behaviors that promote wellness. HR ensures the necessary tools and resources are available. And employees engage with these initiatives, contributing to a culture where well-being is a shared responsibility.

By adopting collaboration at every level, organizations can ensure that wellness isn't just a top-down directive, but a shared value that permeates the entire workforce. Together, we can create a work environment where everyone has the opportunity to thrive.

Tailoring Wellness to Your Organization

Every organization is unique, and the best wellness programs reflect the specific needs and culture of the workplace. Whether you're a large multinational or a small family-run business, wellness initiatives should be customized to fit your team. The key is to **listen to your employees** and design programs that resonate with them. Some may prefer financial wellness workshops, others might benefit from more flexible work schedules or a focus on mental health. The most successful programs will be those that are tailored to the specific challenges and preferences of your workforce.

Wellness doesn't have to look the same in every workplace. The best initiatives are those that align with your organization's values, size, and structure while still addressing the core elements of well-being—mental, physical, and emotional.

Practical Next Steps

As you move forward, here are some tangible steps to help you begin implementing the wellness principles from this book:

1. **Start Small, Dream Big**

    Begin with one wellness initiative—a weekly mindfulness session, a team-building activity, or an employee feedback survey. From there, scale your efforts based on what works and the feedback you receive.

2. **Engage Your Team**

    Involve employees in the process. Ask for their input, listen to their concerns, and tailor programs to fit their needs. Employee engagement ensures your initiatives are meaningful and effective.

3. **Measure Impact**

    Regularly assess the success of your wellness programs. Use surveys, participation rates, and feedback to track progress. Measuring helps you adjust and ensure continued success.

4. **Celebrate Wins**

    Recognize individual and team achievements in wellness. Acknowledge the efforts of those who actively participate in wellness programs and celebrate milestones along the way. This helps build momentum and reinforces the value of wellness in the workplace.

5. **Commit to Consistency**

    Wellness is an ongoing journey. Ensure that wellness programs are continually reviewed and refreshed to stay relevant to employees' needs. Consistency is key to making wellness an integral part of your workplace culture.

A Vision for the Future

Imagine a future where every employee, from entry-level to CEO, feels energized, supported, and valued. A future where work-life balance isn't a goal, but a given. In this future, wellness isn't just a program or a policy—it's a way of life. This is the future we can create, together. By integrating wellness into every aspect of our organizations, we can build workplaces that don't just aim for success—but achieve sustainable, holistic success that benefits employees, teams, and entire communities.

Closing Thoughts: A Lasting Commitment

As Mahatma Gandhi said, *"The best way to find yourself is to lose yourself in the service of others."* When we prioritize wellness, we are not only investing in the well-being of our employees but also creating workplaces that reflect our deepest values of care, respect, and collaboration. This is not just about better business outcomes—it's about building a better world, one workplace at a time.

Your Takeaway Challenge

Set three wellness goals for your workplace or personal life:

- **Immediate Step**: Launch one small wellness initiative in the next month (e.g., organize a wellness check-in or mental health day).
- **Medium-Term Goal**: Develop a strategy for a comprehensive wellness program that addresses both physical and mental health.
- **Long-Term Vision**: Integrate wellness into your organization's core values and long-term strategy.

Commit to taking one actionable step this week and watch how small changes can create ripple effects that impact not only your workplace but your community as well.

Workplace wellness is a movement, and you are at the forefront. Together, let's create workplaces where people aren't just working—they're flourishing.

Share Your Thoughts: Leave a Review

Thank you for accompanying me on this journey through "Workplace Wellness: Balancing Work and Mental Health." I hope you found the strategies and insights within these pages helpful and inspiring as you work towards enhancing wellness in your own workplace.

If this book has made a difference in how you view and implement workplace wellness, I would be grateful if you could take a few minutes to leave a review on Amazon. Your feedback not only supports me as an author but also helps other readers discover and benefit from these practices. Share what you found most useful, and how you plan to apply these ideas in your work environment.

Simply scan the QR code below to visit the book's page and leave your review.

Your voice matters, and sharing your experience can inspire others to make positive changes in their workplaces. Thank you for your support and for contributing to a global conversation on workplace wellness.

www.ingramcontent.com/pod-product-compliance
Lightning Source LLC
Chambersburg PA
CBHW071104240526
45469CB00006BD/2328